# Words in their Places

*Graded Cloze Texts and Comprehension Exercises*

Lynn Hutchinson

HODDER AND STOUGHTON
LONDON SYDNEY AUCKLAND TORONTO

British Library Cataloguing in Publication Data

Hutchinson, Lynn
Words in their places.
1. English language–Composition and exercises
I. Title
428'.2 PE1112

ISBN 0 340 24447 X

First published 1980


Fifth impression 1983


Phototypeset in V.I.P. Baskerville by
Western Printing Services Ltd, Bristol.

Printed in Great Britain for Hodder and Stoughton Educational,
a division of Hodder and Stoughton Ltd,
Mill Road, Dunton Green, Sevenoaks, Kent,
by Biddles Ltd, Guildford, Surrey.

# Contents

An introduction and a key to the cloze texts is available free on application. Please address all applications to **The Primary Editorial Department, Hodder and Stoughton Educational, PO Box 702, Dunton Green, Sevenoaks, Kent, TN13 2YD**, enclosing a large stamped addressed envelope.

# Chairs

How many kinds ___ chair have you sat on? Some chairs have arms ___ so they are called armchairs. Armchairs are often large ___ soft. It is nice to rest in an armchair. ___ is not easy to eat your dinner in ___ armchair. Your elbows bang on the arms. You can ___ get close to the table. Most people like to ___ up to eat their dinners. Dining chairs usually ___ straight backs. Often they have padded seats.

The ___ you use at school do not have padded seats ___ arms. They often have straight backs and hard seats! You ___ more likely to stay awake in a school chair. ___ are just the right height for you to work ___ a desk or table. They are also strong so ___ many pupils can use them before they wear out.

*Now answer these questions in sentences:*

1. What sort of chair is nice and soft?
2. Does a dining chair have arms?
3. Does a school chair have a padded seat?
4. Which two chairs have straight backs?
5. Which chair is best for resting in?
6. What do you call a chair you sit on at meal times?
7. Which chairs are used by many people?
8. Write about your favourite chair. Say what colour and shape it is. Say what you like to do best in it. Draw it.

# Bed Time

Bed time comes at the end of every ____. There are some days when it is nice to ____ to bed. The day before a birthday is one ____ those days. The day before a holiday is another one. ____ is because the sooner you go to bed, ____ sooner the next day comes. When you are ill, ____ often feel better after a long sleep. Then it ____ best to go to bed early. But when you are ____, you wish for a later bed time.

*Now answer these questions in sentences:*

1. What time do you go to bed on a school day?
2. What time do you go to bed in the holidays?
3. When do you like to go to bed early?
4. When do you wish for a later bed time?
5. Do you like to go to bed later or earlier on Christmas Eve? Why?

# Wild Life in Towns

Many people live ___ towns. Many wild creatures live in towns also. These creatures ___ birds and animals and insects. They have learnt to live ___ people.

The plants on railway and canal banks ___ birds, mice, voles, shrews and rabbits. They are hunting grounds ___ hedgehogs, badgers, foxes and squirrels.

The fish in canals attract many ___, like herons and swans.

Rubbish tips supply all sorts of ___ to many wild creatures.

Some animals have ___ pests. Foxes often tear open modern paper dustbins. Mice ___ rats can be a problem.

All these creatures have ___ to adapt to town life.

*Now answer these questions in sentences:*

1. Where are plants found in towns?
2. What creatures feed on the plants?
3. What do swans like about canals?
4. Why do you think wild creatures like rubbish tips?
5. Name three pests mentioned in the text.
6. In what way are the creatures mentioned above different from animals found in the country?

# Ponds

Small ponds can change a lot ___ a year. They may be frozen over in winter. ___ it thaws they may be very full. In ___ hot summer, they may dry up. Only a few ___ can stand changes like these. Here are three of ___ ways creatures find to survive in a small ___.

Water fleas, water bears and fairy shrimps can live ___ small ponds. Their eggs will not die if the ___ dries up. They will stay in the dried mud ___ the pond fills up again.

Midges, horseflies, newts and frogs need ___ be in water for the first part of their lives. ___, when the pond dries up, they fly away or ___ to live on the land.

Water boatmen and water beetles ___ a dry pond and go and find water somewhere ___.

*Now answer these questions in sentences:*

1. Why do small ponds change so much?
2. What is likely to happen to a small pond in winter?
3. What is likely to happen to a small pond in summer?
4. What happens to the eggs of fairy shrimps if the pond dries up?
5. What do newts do if the pond dries up?
6. What do horseflies do when the pond dries up?
7. What do water beetles do when the pond dries up?
8. How many creatures have eggs that will not die in a dry pond?
9. How many creatures only need to live in water for the first part of their lives?
10. Which of these creatures need water in the summer?

# Adders

The only poisonous snake found ___ Britain is the adder. There are ___ adders in Ireland. Legends ___ that Saint Patrick drove all the ___ away.

Adders are about two feet ___. The head of an adder ___ arrow-shaped. The markings on ___ body vary. The background colour can ___ green, brown, grey or cream. ___ are even all black adders! Most ___ have a zig-zag line down ___ backs, and an X or V shape ___ their heads.

In the winter, adders hibernate. ___ like to curl up in cracks ___ the ground about one foot ___. Often forty adders will sleep in the ___ den. They like to ___ lizards, mice, voles and shrews. Bites ___ humans are rarely fatal. The chief ___ of adders is the hedgehog. The ___ kills by biting, then curling ___ a prickly ball, then biting ___, and so on. When the ___ is dead, the hedgehog eats it.

*Now answer these questions in sentences:*

1. How many poisonous types of snake are there in Britain?
2. Why do people say Ireland has not got any poisonous snakes?
3. How long are adders?
4. What do adders do in the winter?
5. What are the most usual background colours?
6. What shape is an adder's head?
7. What markings does an adder usually have?
8. How many adders are often found together?
9. What do adders eat?
10. What eats adders?
11. How do hedgehogs kill adders?
12. If you are bitten by an adder, will you probably die?

# Bird Sounds

There are many different kinds ___ bird. All birds make sounds known as 'calls'. Birds ___ the same sort call to each other. A dove ___ to a dove. A chaffinch calls to a ___. The call of a bird says many things. It ___ warn of an enemy. It can pass on news.

Many ___ also have songs as well as calls. These birds ___ called song birds. When birds sing they tell the world ___ the bird owns that piece of land. They warn ___ other birds. A lark is a song bird. A robin ___ a song bird. A little wren is a song bird ___ a loud song. Very often, if a bird ___ not easy to see, like the wren, it has ___ louder song to make up.

Some birds, like the whitethroat, ___ born able to call and sing. It does ___ have to be taught by its parents. Other birds, ___ the chaffinch, need to be taught to sing ___ their parents. There are some birds who copy other ___. The starling can copy the sounds of many birds. A starling ___ even learnt to copy the ringing of a telephone.

*Now answer these questions in sentences:*

1. What are bird calls?
2. What bird does a dove call to?
3. How do birds pass on news?
4. Can all birds sing?
5. Do song birds have calls as well as songs?
6. Name two song birds.
7. Which birds have the loudest song?
8. Why do birds sing?
9. How does the whitethroat learn to sing?
10. How does the chaffinch learn to sing?
11. Name a bird which copies other birds' songs.
12. Which bird do you like to hear best?

# Beach Weather

The summer day has turned cold. People ___ the beach put on their jerseys, then their ___. The sun-traps become wind-breaks. As the sky gets greyer, the ___ gets colder. Some children run up and down the water's ___, throwing stones. They run and retreat before each wave, careful ___ to get their shoes wet. A woman can be ___ striding along the water's edge, head down. In front of ___ lopes a dog. The beach loses a few people ___ a time. At last it is deserted. The waves ___ on the stones, unseen by human eyes. Only the birds are ___ to witness the harsh moods of the sea.

*Now answer these questions in sentences:*

1. What season is written about?
2. How do the people keep warm?
3. What are sun-traps?
4. Why does the writer say the sun-traps become wind-breaks?
5. What games do the children play?
6. Why does the woman walk with her head down?
7. Why do you think she is out on a day like this?
8. Describe how people leave the beach.
9. After the people are gone, what is left?
10. Who knows the sea best, and why?

# Food We Eat

A lot of the world's rice is ___ in India. Rice ___ are grown in the ___ beside rivers. When the ___ monsoon comes, the rivers overflow ___ the fields. Mud ___ stop the water from draining back into the ___. If the rainy ___ comes late, or not at all, then the ___ won't grow because there is not enough ___. If there is not a good ___, millions of people may ___ of starvation.

Cocoa and coffee both grow on ___. It is the ___ of the cocoa pods which are dried and then ___ to make ___ powder. Coffee cherries have ___ pulp removed in a ___. Inside the cherry are two ___. These are ___ and ground to make ___.

From the oil-palm ___ come two sorts of ___. The oil ___ the flesh is used for machinery. The ___ from the kernel is used ___ soap and margarine.

*Now answer these questions in sentences:*

1. Which country does rice grow in?
2. Where are the fields in which the rice plants are grown?
3. What happens to the rivers in India when it rains?
4. What sort of conditions do rice plants like?
5. What happens to the rice if there is not enough rain?
6. What happens to the people if there is not enough rice?
7. What do coffee, cocoa and oil grow on?
8. Which part of the cocoa pods is used?
9. How is the pulp taken off the coffee cherries?
10. How many beans are there in a coffee cherry?
11. Which part of the cherry is used?
12. How are the cocoa and coffee beans made into powder?
13. Which tree gives two sorts of oil?
14. From which part of the tree comes oil for soap and margarine?
15. From which part of the tree comes oil for machinery?
16. Do any of these foods grow in Britain?
17. Which of these foods is eaten in Britain?
18. How do you think these foods are sent to other countries?

# The Haircut

The boy, with a sinking heart, ___ unwillingly on the stool. His mother wrapped a ___ round him, tucking the ___ down his shirt collar.

'Only the ___, Mum, only the fringe,' he pleaded.

'___ needs thinning for the summer. I'll ___ to do that as well if you ___ to go swimming and play rounders,' ___ his mother. 'Now, do you want ___ the same shape as last time?'

'All ___, but only a little bit. Everybody'll ___. You don't know what it's like. ___ all call after you, and ___ you skin-head.'

'Well, take no ___. Don't they ever get their ___ cut?'

There was no answer as ___ trimmed and snipped away, taking off ___ much as she dared. Only the odd command ___ be heard, telling the boy to ___ up straight, keep his head ___, or keep his chin up. The ___ obeyed these instructions for a few ___ before sinking back into his hunched ___ defeated position.

'There, I think that ___ do. I've had to make it a bit shorter ___ you wanted it, to balance it.'

She ___ the hair off him, and he wriggled ___ the stool to see what damage ___ had done. She thought, as he rushed upstairs ___ the mirror, that she'd made rather a ___ job this time. The ___ suited him, and set off his features. ___ the door opened again. He ___ there, his eyes glinting with ___. 'I hate you,' he said.

*Now answer these questions in sentences:*

1. Which people are in this story?
2. What event is described?
3. Why doesn't the boy want his hair cut?
4. Why does the mother cut the boy's hair?
5. How does the boy sit as it is done?
6. Where does the boy go after she has finished?
7. Why does the mother think she has done a good job?
8. Why do you think the boy makes the last remark?

# Breadmaking

Home-made bread is fun to ___ and delicious to eat. All you ___ is flour, salt, yeast, sugar ___ honey, and butter or oil. You mix the yeast ___ the sugar and add some lukewarm water.* Set this ___ to one side and it ___ start growing. Mix the flour and salt, ___ rub in the butter. If you ___ oil, add it to the lukewarm water. Next add the yeast mixture and some ___ water.

Thoroughly mix all the ___. This part is usually a bit messy, ___ fun! Leave the dough in a bowl for ___ to double in size. Turn it out ___ a board dusted with flour, ___ knead it. You knead by pushing the ___ away from you with the heels ___ your hands. Pick it up, slap ___ round, bash it! Usually, the more kneading you give it, ___ better the bread. Put the ___ into tins, then leave ___ to rise again. Cook it in a hot ___. After half an hour or so you ___ warm, home-made bread.

*Take three-quarters ___ a pint of cold water. Add a quarter of a ___ of boiling water. When the water is mixed ___ these proportions of three ___ one, you have lukewarm water.

*Now answer these questions in sentences:*

1. What ingredients do you need for making bread?
2. What kitchen equipment do you need?
3. What does the yeast do when it is mixed with sugar and water?
4. Which is the messy part?
5. How do you know when to knead the dough?
6. What is kneading?
7. Is it better to knead it a little or a lot?
8. After you've kneaded the dough where should you put it?
9. What happens to the dough then?
10. What proportion of cold to boiling water makes lukewarm water?
11. How long does the bread take to cook?
12. What advantages are there in making your own bread?

# Parks

The first parks were owned ___ kings. They were special areas used for hunting. The kings ___ parks to their nobles as rewards.

In time, hunting ___ given up, and many parks were built on. About two hundred ___ ago, rich people had parks made round ___ stately homes. Often rivers were moved, lakes ___ made, trees planted. Sometimes ruins were specially ___ to make the park look natural.

About a ___ years ago, parks were built in cities and towns ___ the councils. These were for poorer people to exercise ___ amuse themselves.

*Now answer these questions in sentences:*

1. Who owned the first parks?
2. What were the first parks used for?
3. What animals do you think might have been hunted?
4. What happened to many early parks after the hunting was stopped?
5. Why do you think rich people wanted parks round their homes?
6. What sort of things were done to make these parks look natural?
7. Who built the parks in towns and cities?
8. Why did poorer people need parks?
9. What is there to exercise on in the park nearest to you?
10. What is there to amuse you in the park nearest to you?
11. What do you like to do best in a park?
12. What do you think a really good park should have in it?

# Thank You Letter

Dear Aunty Sarah and Uncle Mark,

Thank you ___ much for the record token ___ sent me for my birthday. I ___ really pleased, as I ___ been wanting to buy a ___ for ages, but I didn't ___ enough money. I didn't know which ___ to choose at first, but finally got one ___ the Electric Light Orchestra. ___ you heard of them? I ___ they are great.

___ are you all keeping? How ___ Elizabeth these days? I hope ___ broken ankle is getting better ___ she can walk properly now. We ___ all well, except that Jeremy ___ a cold. Tessa is going ___ have puppies soon. We are very ___ about that.

Mum and Dad ___ their love.

Thank you again ___ remembering my birthday. I am looking ___ to the summer when you come ___ stay.

Love,

Linda.

*Now answer these questions in sentences:*

1. Who wrote the letter?
2. To whom did she write?
3. Why did she write the letter?
4. What had been sent?
5. What did she do with the present?
6. What music does the girl like?
7. Who do you think Elizabeth is?
8. What has been the matter with her?
9. Who is Tessa?
10. What is Linda's family looking forward to?
11. What do Linda's parents send to the uncle and aunt?
12. Who is going to visit whom, and when?

# Night Time

Many people, especially children, are ___ little scared at being out alone ___ night. Everything is deadly quiet. Shadows ___ long and black. They seem to ___ into strange shapes which move ___ you look at them. The slightest sound ___ you jump. Trees seem to tower ___ you. They look quite different ___ moonlight. Often you see glinting and flickering ___ the moonlight catches the leaves. Without ___ daytime colours you feel as ___ you are in a strange ___. The sudden flight of a bat ___ you can be startling or even frightening. ___ you try to hurry the thud ___ your heart is deafening. The echo ___ your footsteps sounds like someone ___ after you.

*Now answer these questions in sentences:*

1. Which people are scared of being out alone at night?
2. How are sounds different at night?
3. What is frightening about shadows?
4. Why do slight sounds frighten you more at night?
5. In what ways are trees different at night?
6. How does your heart sound at night?
7. What do your own footsteps sound like?
8. What do you find the most scary thing about being out alone at night?

# Chapatis

Chapatis are a sort ___ fried bread. They are soft and ___ crisp. They are good for mopping ___ sauces and gravies. Indians make ___ and eat them with rice and curry ___.

Chapatis can be made ___ size. They are very often ___ to elephants. Chapatis fed to ___ are often the size of car wheels. ___ people, chapatis the size ___ a saucer are about right!

___ make chapatis you mix whole wheat flour and salt ___ water. Only add enough water ___ make a soft dough. Knead the ___, then sprinkle it with drops ___ water. Cover it with a cloth. ___ about half an hour, roll the ___ into small balls and then flatten ___ on a floured board. Put them ___ a hot frying pan which ___ been lightly covered in oil. Turn them ___ when the edges start to turn up. ___ for another few seconds. Then, ___ little bubbles in the dough can ___ seen, lift them out of the ___ with tongs. Hold them over ___ hot electric ring or gas flame. ___ will puff right up, then burst. Put ___ on a plate. The rolling ___ cooking should take less ___ a minute for each chapati.

Now ___ them! You can even eat them ___ butter and jam or honey. ___ are still just as nice!

*Now answer these questions in sentences:*

1. What are chapatis made from?
2. With what do they taste nice?
3. Who eats chapatis?
4. What do you do after you have kneaded the dough?
5. What do you roll the dough into?
6. What do you cook them in?
7. When do you turn them over?
8. Why do you think they should be lifted from the pan with tongs?
9. What happens to them when you hold them over heat?
10. How long does the rolling and cooking take?

# The Fairground

In the distance you can ___ the big wheel turning. Aeroplanes zoom ___ the top of the helter-skelter. It ___ not until you are closer ___ you can see the struts which ___ them to the machinery. Music wafts ___ the air. As you get ___, you realise that it is ___ one tune, but several, all tangled.

Then the screams, coming in waves, ___ your ears. At about the same ___ the smell of onions reaches your ___.

Getting closer to the entrance, you ___ groups coming away. Most ___ tired, some look happy. The ___ are sticky and grubby. They drag ___ their parents' hands, not wanting to ___ the excitement. People, eager to get ___, hasten their steps. Round the ___, under the sign, at ___ you're there! The fun of the ___ is yours for the taking!

*Now answer these questions in sentences:*

1. What two things can be seen in the distance?
2. What do you notice about the aeroplanes as you get closer?
3. How do the sounds seem to change as you get nearer?
4. What smell is strongest?
5. Write down any other smells that are very noticeable at a fairground.
6. How are the people leaving and approaching the fairground different?
7. How do the children behave when it is time to go home?
8. Describe your own feelings as you are about to enter a fairground.

# Village Celebrations

The whole of the centre ___ the village had been closed to traffic. Bunting ___ to and fro across the street and ___ the houses. Lining each side ___ the road were groups of people, ___ standing, others on the move. The air ___ filled with subdued conversations, except ___ the odd loud jolly remark. It ___ obvious that the procession was long overdue. ___ crowd, however, did not seem ___, and actually appeared to be enjoying ___ delay.

At last, over the loudspeaker, ___ the news that the procession was ___ its way. Sure enough, rounding the ___ at the end of the street could ___ seen the leading car, headlights on. ___ it came the floats, flaunting flags ___ flowers. Decorated bicycles and tricycles ___ each side of the procession. ___ the back could be seen the tossing heads ___ horses. As the floats drew ___, the crowd cheered and stopped, and ___ again for the next. It was ___ the way hedgerow grass swirls especially ___ each passing car.

*Now answer these questions in sentences:*

1. How was the village decorated?
2. Where were the people standing?
3. What were they waiting for?
4. What was the first indication that the procession was near?
5. What led the procession?
6. With what were the floats decorated?
7. Where were the cycles?
8. What came last?
9. How did the crowds react to each float?
10. What does the writer mean by the image in the last sentence?

# Football Report

United's manager, Steve Donald, has drawn another blank ___ week in his efforts to strengthen ___ playing staff ready for the challenge ___ the second division.

Donald, ___ search in the transfer market was temporarily halted ___ his excursion to Southport with ___ youth team, reopened negotiations this ___, but met with little success.

'I ___ to a First Division club on Monday ___ a young striker, but there is ___ doing yet. I got a similar response ___ I tried another couple of clubs later ___ the week,' he said. 'There's nothing much on the transfer list at the ___.'

One piece of good news for ___ this week concerned defender Phil Stewart. His case ___ up before an F.A. Disciplinary Commission ___ he had collected twenty points. But ___ escaped with a warning as to ___ future conduct which means that United ___ start the season free ___ suspension worries.

*Now answer these questions in sentences:*

1. Who is United's manager?
2. What division is United in now?
3. What division will they be in next season?
4. What has the manager been trying to do all week?
5. Has the manager succeeded in his task?
6. Where had the manager been that week?
7. Who travelled with him, and why?
8. Why is the manager not meeting with success?
9. Who from the team has been in trouble this week?
10. Who has dealt with his case?
11. Why has he been in trouble?
12. What was the outcome of the case?

# Oil

Many millions of years ___ most of the land was ___ in water. Now, most of these ___ have dried up. Countless tiny sea creatures, ___ of flesh and bone, live in ___ sea. When they die, ___ bodies fall to the ocean floor. A ___ time ago there were so many, ___ slowly their bodies collected ___ layers on the sea bed. ___ time went on, their bodies were slowly ___ under mud and soil. Eventually, stone ___ rock also covered them. Under ___ pressure of the rock, the oil from ___ bodies oozed into the stones ___ the ground. This oil is called petroleum oil, and ___ millions of years to form.

The oil ___ actually in the rock, not in a ___ between layers of rocks. This is ___ some rocks are porous. That means ___ they will soak up liquid. ___ example of a porous rock ___ chalk. Lime and sandstone are ___ porous. Rocks which do not ___ up liquid are called non-porous rocks. Flint ___ granite are non-porous rocks.

Oil is found ___ porous rocks, such as ___, chalk, and sandstone. It is trapped in porous rocks ___ layers of non-porous rock. On top ___ the oil there is often gas ___ oil, which has also been ___ in the porous rock.

*Now answer these questions in sentences:*

1. What has happened to much of the water that used to cover the earth?
2. What happened to the bodies of the sea creatures?
3. What were their bodies made of?
4. What covered the bodies of the sea creatures?
5. What caused the oil to ooze into the stones?
6. How long did it take the oil to form?
7. What is often on top of the oil?
8. What sort of rock soaks up oil?
9. What is non-porous rock?
10. What type of rock is the oil trapped between?
11. Is the oil in the rock, or in a pool between the rocks?
12. What is the proper name for rock oil?

# The Cottage

This is how you find the ___.

Drive up the single ___ minor road for one mile. Stop ___ the telephone box above ___ bridge. Open the gate ___ the right, and drive for half a mile ___ the fields. This gate is ___ PLEASE CLOSE THE ___.

Follow the car track ___ the brow of the hill. ___ carefully as on the left ___ is a steep drop to ___ river. You can see the ___ for the last couple of hundred ___, nestled into the hills.

The cottage ___ old and grey, an ___ slate-miner's cottage, with a walled ___ in front. ___ is to keep out the sheep ___ you will find everywhere. ___ name is on the gate, 'Tyn-y-cornel', which means 'house in the corner'. ___ will find the key ___ the mat. Enjoy your ___.

*Now answer these questions in sentences:*

1. Which country do you think the cottage is in, and why?
2. How far altogether is the cottage from the main road?
3. What would you have to do if you met a car on the minor road?
4. How do you know which telephone box to stop at?
5. On which side of the road is the gate with a notice?
6. What is on the other side of the gate?
7. Can you see the cottage from the gate?
8. On which side of the track should you be careful, and why?
9. For how far can you see the cottage before you reach it?
10. Why do you think the cottage is called 'Tyn-y-cornel'?
11. What do you know of the history of the cottage?
12. What do you think the cottage is now used for?

# Magnets

There are many different ___ of magnet. Some are bar-shaped. ___ are called bar magnets. ___ are U-shaped. They are ___ U magnets. Some are horseshoe ___. They are called ___ magnets. But whatever shape ___ is, a magnet is strongest ___ its ends. The ends of a ___ will pick up anything made ___ iron. Pins and needles can ___ picked up. Magnets will even ___ through cloth or paper.

If you ___ a bar magnet on a string, ___ will always swing to ___ north. Compasses are magnets. That is ___ they are used to show ___ way is north. If you know ___ north is, you can work ___ all the other directions. ___ are used by people who ___ to know which direction ___ are going in. Sailors, pilots, ___ walkers all use compasses.

A battery ___ turn a piece of iron ___ a magnet. When an electric current ___ passed through the iron, other things ___ stick to it. If you disconnect ___ battery, the magnet stops ___. Electromagnets are used in scrap ___ to pick up heavy loads. More ___ is used, of course, and ___ of a small piece of iron, ___ is a big iron plate. ___ switching the electricity on and ___ the iron plate can pick ___ and drop heavy loads of ___.

Electromagnets are found ___ bells, televisions and engines. They ___ to make work easier.

*Now answer these questions in sentences:*

1. What shape are magnets?
2. Which part of the magnet is strongest?
3. Which direction will a magnet on a string point in?
4. How can you work out the other directions if you only know north?
5. What do we call a magnet used for direction finding?
6. Who uses compasses?
7. What passes from a battery in a simple electromagnet?
8. How can you stop some iron from being a magnet in a simple electromagnet?
9. Who uses strong electromagnets?
10. Where do you find electromagnets?

# Milking a Cow

Milking a ___ is a very pleasant job. It ___ a job you can not ___. The more you hurry, the slower ___ will be. You need lots ___ time, and a quiet mind. A ___ can tell if you are nervous ___ impatient. If you are ___ quiet and peaceful she will ___ let down her milk easily. Every milkmaid ___ that!

You will ___ milkmaids talking and singing ___ they milk.

Recently ___ was a report in the newspapers ___ cows and milking. It said that on farms ___ the cowmen knew their ___ well, they got more ___. But where the cowmen don't know one ___ from another, and do ___ talk to them, less milk ___ given.

Most milkmaids would ___ be surprised at that ___!

*Now answer these questions in sentences:*

1. Why do you get less milk if you hurry?
2. What can a cow tell about a milkmaid?
3. What is the best frame of mind to be in to milk successfully?
4. What do milkmaids often do to relax their cows?
5. Where was the report on milking?
6. What did the report have to say about cowmen who knew their cows?
7. What did the report have to say about cowmen who did not know their cows?
8. Do you think milkmaids would agree or disagree with the report?
9. The first two paragraphs are about milking by hand. Under what conditions do you think hand milking would be an advantage?
10. The third paragraph is about milking by machine. Under what conditions would machine milking be an advantage?
11. Say where you think your milk comes from, who delivers it, and whether you think the cow was machine or hand milked.

# Growing a Stone

One day, the boys' mother arrived ___ with some strange looking fruit. ___ outside was green and knobbly, ___ you didn't eat that. The ___ was cream and smooth, and it ___ a huge stone. By the time the boys had ___ eating the fruit, they were beginning ___ quite like it. They liked holding ___ fruit in their hands best, and eating it ___ a teaspoon.

Their mother ___ that these fruits were called avocado pears. ___ said that the stones could grow ___ trees which would look nice. ___ none of them were sure what ___ do next, they looked it ___ in a book. The book said that you ___ pierce the stone in three places. Then matchsticks ___ be put in the holes, and the ___ arrangement balanced over a glass of water. One of ___ boys put the sharp end ___ the water. The other boy put ___ blunt end in the ___. This was to see ___ end grew best. Then ___ waited.

___ about two months, one of the ___ started to send down a root. ___ a shoot appeared. Just as they were thinking ___ putting it in soil, the cat ___ on the window sill and knocked it ___. That was the end of the ___ avocado plant!

The second one ___ a root, then a shoot. It was then ___ in a huge pot in case ___ decided to become a tree! It ___ now growing well, with lots of ___. The only trouble is, the boys ___ not remember whose it is, or ___ it had the sharp end or ___ end down!

*Now answer these questions in sentences:*

1. What fruit was brought home?
2. What did it look like?
3. How was it eaten?
4. Did the boys like it?
5. How did they know what to do with it?
6. Describe what had to be done to the stone to make it grow.
7. What happened to the first stone?
8. What happened to the second stone?
9. Should the avocado have the blunt end or the sharp end in water?
10. Why was it put in a large pot?

# In Loco Parentis

Parents can ___ their children more or less ___ they like. They may not harm ___ children of course. If they ___ neglectful or cruel the children can ___ taken away from them. It is ___ that parents love their children and ___ be responsible for them. Parents ___ their children about good and bad, as ___ as how to look after themselves. ___ helps them to grow up ___, in all sorts of ways. However, ___ do not always agree with each ___ over what is the best thing to ___. For example, some parents smack ___ children, others do not.

Problems only arise ___ the children are taken away ___ their parents by other adults. ___ law, the other adults must act 'in loco parentis'. ___ are Latin words which ___ 'in place of parents'. But which ___ have the adults got to replace? ___ are all different!

Every day, all ___ the country, children are taken away ___ their parents. This is, of course, ___ they go to school! The adults ___ school have to act with as ___ care as the most careful ___. By law they are ___ to do so.

*Now answer these questions in sentences:*

1. Who decides how parents should bring up their children?
2. What may parents not do to their children?
3. What sort of things do parents teach their children?
4. What sort of things do parents disagree with each other about?
5. When do other adults take the children from their parents?
6. How does the law expect these other adults to behave?
7. Why is a school expected to do more than just teach children?
8. How does it happen that sometimes a school expects children to behave in a different way from when they are at home?

# The Year

There are ____ seasons in a year. The year ____ also divided into twelve ____. Some months have 31 ____, some have ____ days, and February has either 28 ____ 29 days.

Altogether there ____ 365 days in a year, and 366 ____ in a leap year. In a leap ____ the extra day is added ____ the end of February. Leap ____ happen because there are really $365\frac{1}{4}$ ____ in a year. All ____ quarters are added up until ____ are enough of them to ____ a whole day. It takes ____ years to make the extra day.

As ____ are usually 52 weeks ____ day in a year, in a ____ year there are 52 weeks and ____ days. If Christmas is on a Monday, then ____ following year it will be ____ a Tuesday. That is ____ it is 52 weeks and one day later. But ____ that year was a leap ____, then Christmas would ____ 52 weeks and two days ____, which would make it Wednesday. ____ would have been missed out. We ____ have leaped a day. ____ is why we call every fourth ____ a leap year, because it is one ____ longer.

*Now answer these questions in sentences:*

1. How many days are there really in a year?
2. What do we do with all the quarter days?
3. Which month is the extra day added to?
4. How many days are there in a leap year?
5. If your birthday is on a Thursday this year, what day would it be on next year?
6. Why do we call it a leap year?
7. Starting from today, write out what day this date falls on for the next six years.

# Measuring Glass

Learning how to cut glass ___ a tricky and nerve-racking business. ___ you start, you have got to know ___ much glass to cut.

___ of all, you measure exactly the size ___ the frame in which you want to ___ glass. You should measure to within three millimetres, as a good fit ___ vital. A loose window pane rattles and is ___ likely to break. A pane that ___ too big just has to be cut to size ___ you do double the work! It is always ___ to measure accurately in ___ first place. You should also ___ the same ruler to measure the glass ___ you use to measure the frame. ___ often helps to put a pencil mark ___ the ruler to make sure you get it ___. I once cut 24 panes 3 mm too big on ___ sides as a result of faulty ___. That is a mistake it would be ___ to repeat!

*Now answer these questions in sentences:*

1. What two words does the writer use to describe learning to cut glass?
2. Before you cut the glass what must you do?
3. How exact must your measuring be?
4. If you cut the pane too small, what happens?
5. If you cut the pane too big, what do you have to do?
6. Why do you think the writer tells you to use the same ruler for measuring the glass and frame?
7. What do you think the writer had to do with the panes he measured wrongly?
8. Why do you think the writer thinks measuring is so important?

# Railways

The railways changed the way this country looked more ___ any other invention.

Engines can only go ___ very gentle slopes. Embankments were built on low ground. Cuttings ___ made through high ground. This was to keep the track ___ level as possible. Bridges and viaducts were also ___ to keep the railways away from roads and rivers.

Cities also ___ with the coming of the railways. Because lots of people and goods ___ moving from one place to another, warehouses and stations ___ to be built. Hotels were built for the visitors. Sheds were ___ for the engines, as well as all sorts ___ track.

*Now answer these questions in sentences:*

1. Which invention changed the country most?
2. Why do railway tracks need to be level?
3. What was built if the ground was too low for the railway?
4. How did the railway go over hilly land?
5. What was built to keep railways separate from other traffic?
6. Why were warehouses built next to railways?
7. Who uses stations and hotels?
8. What had to be built for the engines?
9. Can you name anything to do with railways near you? You might be able to think of a bridge or signal box or track. Say where it is.

# The Sahara Desert

Of all the deserts ___ the world, the Sahara desert is the most well known. ___ word 'Sahara' comes from the Arab word for 'emptiness'. The Sahara ___ stretches for $3\frac{1}{2}$ million square miles. It is mainly sand ___ rock. Only part of the desert is made up ___ sand dunes. They are blown about by the ___ and keep changing their shape. In the middle ___ the Sahara desert are rocky mountains. Some of these ___ used to be volcanoes.

People crossing the desert go ___ one oasis to another. An oasis is formed where ___ is some water. Date palms, orange, lemon and lime trees ___ by the water. Vegetables are also grown.

At one time only camels ___ cross the Sahara. This was because they could store ___ food and water in their bodies to last ___ days. Now, the desert can be crossed ___ car. As each oasis is 200–300 miles apart, a breakdown can ___ dangerous.

*Now answer these questions in sentences:*

1. What does the word 'Sahara' mean?
2. Why do you think the Arabs gave it that name?
3. How big is the Sahara desert?
4. What are heaps of sand called?
5. How do we know it is windy in the Sahara?
6. What is in the middle of the Sahara?
7. What did the mountains used to be?
8. What is an oasis?
9. What grows at an oasis?
10. Why are camels used to cross the desert?
11. What else can cross the desert?
12. Why do you think a breakdown could be dangerous?

# Fibre Tip Pens

The first pen was probably a piece ___ reed, or rush stem. Since then, we have had pens made ___ quills, metal nibs, and ball points. Modern ___ now have fibre tips, rather ___ the first pens which were invented.

___ year, over a hundred million pens are ___. They now come in bright ___, not just blue or black.

You can ___ a fibre tip pen for any purpose, for writing ___ drawing. ___ pens have fine lines, whereas drawing pens make ___ lines.

In the middle of a fibre ___ pen is a long piece of material soaked in ___. As ink is rubbed off the tip, more is ___ up from the middle to take ___ place.

Some pens will ___ for 500 feet before being used up. Others ___ write for 2,000 feet before running ___.

If you leave off the ___ of your pen, you will lose at ___ one fifth of the ink in a month. With some pens ___ can lose three quarters of the ink by ___ off the pen top.

Some pens have screw ___, others just push on. If the top ___ off in your pocket, you ___ have a nasty mess.

All fibre tip pens have tips ___ get broader as you write, but ___ pens have tips which broaden ___ easily than others. This can be a nuisance ___ you choose a pen that writes ___ a fine line, but which spreads quickly so that you can ___ make a fine line any ___.

*Now answer these questions in sentences:*

1. Describe the first pens.
2. Why are modern pens like the first pens?
3. How many pens are sold every year?
4. For what purposes do people buy fibre tips?
5. How does the ink reach the point of a fibre tip?
6. What distances can fibre tips cover?
7. Why should you always keep the top on?
8. What happens to the tips of fibre tip pens as you write?
9. Which tops are most likely to come off in your pocket?
10. How should you look after your fibre tip?

# Islam

A Muslim believes there is one God, and ___ name is Allah. Mohammed was ___ prophet. The Archangel Gabriel dictated the holy ___ of the Muslims to Mohammed over a ___ of many years. This holy book is ___ the Koran. It is about the same length ___ the Christians' New Testament. The Koran ___ also like the Old Testament, in that ___ lays down rules which govern a believer's ___ life. Also, stories in the Bible ___ the Koran are often about the same prophets, like Abraham ___ Moses.

The word Koran ___ 'recitation'. It is called this ___ it was a telling by Mohammed of ___ he had found out about Allah and ___ he wanted people to behave. There ___ five great beliefs, called the Five Pillars ___ Islam. Islam is the name of the religion in ___ Muslims believe. The five beliefs are:–

(1) Belief ___ Allah.
(2) Prayer five times ___ day.
(3) Charity.
(4) Fasting. To celebrate ___ month when God first spoke ___ Mohammed, Muslims do not eat or drink ___ dawn to sunset for the whole of ___ month. [This fasting month is ___ Ramadan. At the end of the ___ there is a festival.]
(5) Pilgrimage. All ___ must try to make a pilgrimage ___ Mecca, their holy city.

*Now answer these questions in sentences:*

1. What is the Muslim name for God?
2. Who was his prophet?
3. What is the name of the holy book of the Muslims?
4. How is it similar to the Old Testament?
5. Who dictated the holy book to Mohammed?
6. What does Koran mean?
7. What are the great beliefs of Islam?
8. How often should a Muslim pray?
9. What is Ramadan?
10. Why is Mecca important to Muslims?

# Summer Evening

It is a summer evening ____ June. The sun is sinking lower ____ the sky, but there is still a ____ warmth in the sun. Keen gardeners finish ____ watering, now the heat and glare ____ the day is over. Drifting ____ fences and hedges can be heard the ____ of hoes in soil. From another ____ comes the repeated rolling sound ____ a lawn mower. The ____ chatter in the trees as they settle ____ the night. The scent of honeysuckle ____ wallflowers hangs in the ____. Next door's child is ____ the piano. The sound drifts ____ the road until at last he ____. On the other ____, Radio One competes with the ____ at first, and then continues victorious, ____ the piano is silent.

Behind open ____ and drawn curtains children lie in warm ____ waiting for sleep, reading ____ day dreaming. It is summer ____ again.

*Now answer these questions in sentences:*

1. What month is this passage about?
2. Name three activities that gardeners are engaged in.
3. What smell can be detected?
4. What musical sounds can be heard?
5. Name three other summer sounds mentioned.
6. Where are the children now?
7. What are the children doing?
8. Can you describe any other sounds typical of a summer evening?

# Great White Shark

The great white shark has attacked more people ___ any other shark. It can be ___ all over the world. It can ___ to 40 feet long, and ___ 20 thousand pounds, or 9 tons. Its ___ is 32 miles per hour.

It has a ___ strong sense of smell. For instance, ___ can smell one drop of blood ___ 10 million drops of sea water. It does not ___ any ears, but can hear for hundreds ___ feet with organs inside its body. ___ sight is also good, and it is ___ at seeing shapes rather than details, even ___ dim light. Its eyes shine in the ___, like a cat's.

Along its body it ___ a lateral line, which can detect vibrations ___ the water from a long way ___. The shark can tell from faint movements ___ the water, where something to eat ___, how far away it is, and ___ fast it is moving.

Because a shark ___ so heavy, it would sink if it did ___ keep swimming. It also has to ___ moving water flowing into its mouth and out ___ its gills all the time. This is ___ oxygen is taken out of the water in ___ gills, and the shark needs oxygen ___ keep alive. Therefore, great white sharks have ___ swim day and night so that ___ can breathe oxygen and so that they do ___ sink.

Great white sharks have eggs ___ hatch inside their bodies. The first egg ___ hatch in each of the two special places inside ___ mother first of all eats up all the eggs. The baby sharks stay inside ___ mother for 2 years. When they are born at ___, they have to be careful ___ sometimes the mother eats them.

*Now answer these questions in sentences:*

1. How long does a great white shark grow?
2. How fast can it go?
3. Give an example of how well a shark can smell.
4. What is a great white shark best at seeing?
5. Give three things a great white shark can tell from its lateral line.
6. Give two reasons why a shark has to keep swimming.
7. How long does it take for a baby shark to be born?
8. What does the first egg to hatch do?
9. How far can a great white shark hear?
10. Which shark has attacked most people?

# Eight-legged Pets

There are lots of reasons ___ not owning cats and dogs. ___ foul gardens and pavements, parks and ___ fields. Their excrement often contains dangerous parasites ___ can cause blindness in children. They ___ huge amounts of food, including whales ___ horses. They can give you rabies. ___ bite, scratch, and sometimes kill, especially children. They ___ you fleas and ticks, and they ___ you awake at night with ___ and caterwauling. On the other hand, they ___ be good company, and keep down mice and ___ pests.

The latest fashion is now ___ tarantula spiders. They are just ___ cuddly and friendly as dogs and ___, and they chase small insects ___ mice. Some varieties of tarantula are ___ poisonous. They are clean, quiet, and cheap ___ look after. They like being around humans, and ___ to the hand of their owners. They ___ between £5.50 and £28, depending on which ___ you have. The most popular are ___ Mexican Redlegs, which are large (20–25 cm leg span), friendly, and ___ beautiful colours.

*Now follow these instructions:*

1. Make *two* lists, with a heading for each list, showing the advantages and disadvantages of keeping dogs and cats as pets. Use *only* the ideas in this passage.
2. Now write down all the advantages of having a spider instead of a cat or dog. Use *only* the ideas in this passage.
3. Write down all the disadvantages you can think of in having a spider for a pet.
4. Which do you prefer? Why?
5. In what ways does the writer try to persuade you that spiders are better pets than cats and dogs?

# Fruit Growing

Kent is a very fertile county. That ____ that many of the foods we ____ grow well in that area. In the northern ____ of the county there are many orchards ____ fruit is grown.

The first fruits ____ ripen are cherries and gooseberries. These are ____ and sent by lorry or rail ____ New Covent Garden in London. There, wholesalers ____ miles around buy boxes of fruit ____ take back to their shops.

Raspberries ____ blackcurrants follow on from the earlier ____. While they are being ____, apples, pears and plums slowly ____ on the trees.

Different fruits ____ well in different areas. Most soft ____ like a warm and sheltered place. Even ____ and pears, which are much hardier ____ other fruits can still be damaged ____ late spring frosts. That is why ____ are not many apple orchards ____ the North of England, except in very sheltered ____.

*Now answer these questions in sentences:*

1. Which county is mentioned in this passage?
2. Which part of the county has many orchards?
3. Which fruits ripen first?
4. Which fruits ripen last?
5. What happens to the fruit when it is picked?
6. What do wholesalers do with the fruit?
7. What sort of weather do soft fruits like?
8. Which two fruits are the most hardy?
9. Why are there not many orchards in the North of England?
10. Name six fruits that are *not* grown in England.

# Hair Weaving

A new way ___ covering up baldness is hair weaving. ___ advertisements say, 'it is so light, easy ___ comfortable to wear that you can ___ it.'

How is hair weaving ___ from a hairpiece? You usually ___ to take a hairpiece off at ___. People often worry about ___ coming off at other times. Some___ find fiddling with sticky tape ___ nuisance when you put it on ___ take it off. A hairpiece usually costs ___ £50.

Hairweaving is very simple. ___ are two ways of doing it. The ___ and most common way is just to stich ___ ordinary hairpiece into your hair. The second way is ___ tie some short cords from ___ side of a bald head ___ the other. This is rather ___ darning. Hair weaving costs about £200. You have ___ to go back to have the weave tightened every six weeks. ___ visit costs £5–£10.

It ___ hurts to have the hairpiece ___ into your hair. Some people ___ wearing a hair weave painful. Some find it very difficult ___ wash.

A recent survey showed ___ about 37% of people with hair weaves ___ it very successful. Another 19% ___ fairly pleased. 5% were not pleased. 37% found ___ very unsuccessful.

*Now answer these questions in a sentence:*

1. What two ways are there of covering up baldness?
2. What two ways are there of hair weaving?
3. What do people not like about wearing a hairpiece?
4. What do people not like about having a hair weave?
5. What is the difference in cost between having a hairpiece and hair weave?
6. What percentage of people altogether found hair weaving very or fairly successful?
7. What percentage of people altogether found hair weaving very or fairly unsuccessful?
8. Were more people pleased or displeased?
9. Do you think what the advertisements say is truthful?
10. If you went bald, what would you do? Why?

# Letter of Complaint

The Manager,
Bridgwater Stores,
Southwich.
Dear ___,

On Friday I ___ a sixteen inch brown zip ___ my jacket. On Saturday I had ___ put in my jacket, and on Tuesday ___ broke. This morning ___ took the jacket ___ to ask for ___ replacement zip. An assistant said it ___ to be cut out of the jacket and ___ back to the manufacturer. I did ___ have time to do it at ___ time as I had to get back ___ work. I have been told ___ under the Trades Description Act, you ___ responsible for the goods you ___. It is up to you to ___ it up with the manufacturer. ___ the meantime, you have sold me a faulty ___. I have already suffered enough inconvenience ___ having to wait weeks just to ___ a new zip. I cannot even ___ my jacket.

I think you should have ___ the zip immediately. As it is, ___ stand to lose a very ___ customer. I would be grateful ___ you would reply to this ___, and comment on the treatment I ___ received.

Yours ___,
N. O. Coat.

*Now answer these questions in sentences:*

1. To whom did this customer write?
2. Why did the customer return with the jacket?
3. What did the assistant tell the customer?
4. To what Act of Parliament did the customer refer?
5. Under this Act, who is responsible for the goods which are sold?
6. Why did the customer feel that the shop should have replaced the goods immediately?
7. In your view, should the shop or the manufacturer replace the zip?
8. Why do you think the customer has written this letter?
9. What action do you think the customer expects?
10. If you were the Manager, what would you do now?

# Kittens

For a couple of weeks ___ our cat was due to have kittens, she was so enormous ___ she looked as though she ___ burst! She didn't make nests in drawers or airing cupboards, ___ everyone told us she would. Maybe, because ___ was her first litter, she ___ not know what to do herself!

We ___ a box for her, and put ___ material in it. One day, ___ we came home, we looked ___ the box. There were five assorted scraps ___ fur, looking more like tousled guinea pigs ___ kittens! The cat lay there contentedly, ___ all the time. She was ___ attentive mother and hardly ___ left them in the first weeks.

Sadly, however, ___ a few days the two tabbies died, followed ___ the grey kitten. When we found it ___ the morning, cold and stiff, the ___ wouldn't let us take it ___ of the box. She tried ___ several hours to lick it back ___ life.

At six weeks ___ the two black kittens are full ___ fun. They pounce on their mother, ___ her food while she sits patiently by; and, ___ course, they fight! We have the feeling ___ she won't be entirely sorry ___ they are old enough to ___ us. Life will be ___ peaceful then.

*Now answer these questions in sentences:*

1. What preparations did the cat make for her kittens?
2. How many litters had she had before?
3. What did the people do to prepare for the kittens?
4. How many kittens were born?
5. What colour, and how many of each colour, were the kittens?
6. How many survived?
7. In what two ways did the cat react when the grey kitten died?
8. When they are six weeks old, how do the kittens treat their mother?
9. In what way will the household be different when the kittens leave?
10. In what ways does the cat show she is a good mother?

# Summer Migrants

Birds migrating to Britain ___ the summer begin to arrive about mid-March. The chiff-chaff and wheatear ___ first, the cuckoo, the warbler, ___ last the spotted flycatcher, in May. Every ___ there are letters in the newspapers about ___ first hearing of the chiff-chaff, the willow warbler, ___ black-cap and the cuckoo, or the first ___ of the swallow, the swift and turtle dove. These ___ the birds that come with summer. To ___ summer birds, Britain is their ___ home.

Every spring ___ 100 million land birds take up territories ___ Britain's 57 million acres, build nests, and ___ their young. Each spring, also, millions of sea birds come ___ our shores and cliffs to breed. Of all ___ birds, 133 species are resident. They breed ___ and are found throughout the winter. These ___ thrushes, blackbirds, sparrows, finches and tits. Every ___ another 52 species come ___ the warmer countries.

In ___ then, begins the great trek home. Birds ___ out on the long flight that ___ them to their breeding grounds. These prodigious flights do ___ pass unobserved. Spring and early ___ are the bird watcher's high noon.

*Now answer these questions in sentences:*

1. Why do the birds mentioned come to Britain?
2. When do they arrive?
3. How many land birds come for the summer?
4. How many species of bird are resident here, summer and winter?
5. How many species come for the summer only?
6. Which two birds come first, and when?
7. Which two birds come last, and when?
8. Name eight birds that migrate to Britain for the summer.
9. Name five birds here all year round.
10. What time of year do bird watchers like most?

# Malaria

Malaria is a disease. Mosquitoes ___ not cause this disease, they only ___ it to other people. They do ___ by sucking the blood of a ___ with the disease. They pass ___ the disease by biting someone else. Then that person ___ ill, because he has had the parasites causing the disease ___ on to him in the bite of the ___.

This disease ___ to cause the death of thousands of ___ every year in hot, tropical ___. Only one sort of mosquito ___ spread the disease, and ___ mosquito is only found in hot, ___ regions.

Nowadays, people who are sick with ___ are treated with a drug ___ quinine, and other more modern ___. Quinine is a very strong drug, ___ it helps to make people with malaria ___ better. Unfortunately, it can cause damage to the heart, and a person with a ___ heart cannot take it. That is why ___ has been a search for drugs which ___ cure malaria without ___ the heart.

A person with ___ suddenly feels cold, and soon ___ is tormented by a burning heat. Sometimes ___ attacks of fever return a ___ days or years later, perhaps long ___ the person has come back from ___ countries.

*Now answer these questions in sentences:*

1. What is malaria?
2. How do mosquitoes pass it on?
3. What causes the disease?
4. In which part of the world is there most malaria?
5. Do all mosquitoes pass on the disease?
6. How many people used to die a year of malaria?
7. How do you know you have got malaria?
8. Does malaria clear up quickly?
9. Which drug is most commonly used against malaria?
10. What is the disadvantage of quinine?
11. Are there alternatives to quinine?
12. Can you think of any way to stop the spread of malaria?

# Cutting Glass

When cutting a piece of glass, ___ are several points to watch. Always hold ___ glass cutter so that it is pressed straight ___ (not on the slant), and cut the glass ___ making one thin sharp scratch. Do ___ try to make the first scratch deeper by going ___ it again. This is because the glass cutter ___ slip out of the first cut and make ___ one beside it. Where there are two ___ close together, the glass may not crack cleanly. Always ___ to make one long cut rather than ___ shorter ones.

If you cut your shape ___ the corner of a larger piece ___ glass, you will only have to cut ___ sides, but you will have to cut ___ glass right across from edge to ___. Using the glass cutter and a ruler ___ the two sides of your shape ___ the glass. Then move the glass so ___ one of the scored lines is ___ line with the edge of the table. This line ___ also be right above the edge. The ___ to be snapped off will project ___ the edge of the table. Holding the glass on the table firmly, ___ the other hand snap the glass ___ along the cut by pressing ___ outer edge firmly ___ evenly towards the floor. Turning the glass, repeat ___ the other side.

*Now answer these questions in sentences:*

1. How should you hold the glass cutter?
2. Why should you not try to make the scratch deeper?
3. Why should you always try to make only one long cut?
4. What sort of furniture should you work on?
5. Where on the table should you position the scored line?
6. Which piece of glass sticks over the edge of the table?
7. How do you keep the glass on the table down?
8. Do you snap the glass downwards or upwards?
9. Which part do you think would be the most nerve-wracking?
10. What danger to a person do you think there could be in cutting glass?

# Sweeteners

To get sugar, sugar cane ___ stewed with water and strained, leaving ___ dark, sticky liquid called molasses. Molasses ___ like black treacle, has a strong ___ and is sweet. Further boiling makes ___ sugar crystallise and it can be sieved ___. This is known ___ raw sugar, and it is dark brown. Lighter brown sugars ___ been washed to remove the molasses ___. Golden syrup can be made by ___ processing. Pure refined sugar is white, ___ sweet, and has lost all its nutritional ___.

Sugar beet is also used to ___ refined sugar.

As sugar ___ a preservative, it keeps indefinitely. ___ can also be sweetened ___ honey, which of course comes ___ bees. The honey can be processed, ___ unprocessed. Honey that is unprocessed ___ tiny bits of wax and pollen. ___ is processed by beating, blending ___ homogenising. Bees only make clear ___, but it does eventually crystallise. Cold ___ honey crystallise, and each honey crystallises ___ a different way. You can ___ honey set by 'seeding', which means ___ a spoonful of set honey, stirring it ___ the runny honey, and leaving it ___ a cool place for a few days. It ___ have crystals the same size ___ the honey used for 'seeding'. ___ make set honey become clear, just leave ___ in a warm place.

Honey ___ indefinitely without having to be sealed. ___ found in the Pyramids was still unspoiled ___ three thousand years. The flavour varies, ___ on the flowers used by the ___. It contains many essential nutrients, ___ a mild sedative, and a powerful ___ soothing antiseptic.

*Now answer these questions in sentences:*

1. What is molasses?
2. What is raw sugar?
3. How is pure refined sugar made?
4. How is honey processed?
5. How can clear honey be made to set?
6. How can set honey be made clear?
7. Why does the flavour of honey vary?
8. What are the keeping properties of both honey and sugar?
9. What other properties does honey have?
10. Which of these would you describe as a natural sweetener, and why?

# Mirages

Have you ever noticed water ___ on the road on a hot day, ___ when you get up to it, ___ road is quite dry? Your eyes seem to ___ played a trick on you! When the air nearest the road ___ heated it rises upwards to where it ___ cooler. It rises in the same way ___ smoke from the fire rises upwards. Therefore, on a ___ in summer, you get hot ___ rising.

We expect light to travel ___ straight lines. Think of a torch beam. However, light can ___ bent. Spectacle glass ___ light, usually when the lenses ___ our eyes are not doing it ___ enough. A spoon standing in a glass ___ water does not look straight. Likewise, ___ air can bend light. When ___ air is rising, then the light rays ___ bent.

Instead of light from ___ sky falling on the road ___ the usual way, the light from the ___ is bent along the road. As ___moves through hot air, it is bent, ___ is what we call refraction. ___ eyes find all this a ___ difficult. Instead of seeing a refraction ___ the light from the sky, our eyes ___ it is a reflection on ___ road. Then, instead of a reflection of ___ sky, our brains think of water, which is what ___ usually reflected on the road; and so we think we ___ water being reflected on the road!

___ we come across something strange, and mistakenly think ___ are seeing something else, we call what ___ see a mirage. So ___ we see water on a dry road, we ___ really seeing a mirage.

*Now answer these questions in sentences:*

1. How do we know light usually travels in straight lines?
2. What substances bend light?
3. What does hot air do?
4. Why do you only see mirages on a hot day?
5. What is bent along the road on a hot day?
6. What does refraction do to light?
7. What do our eyes think refraction is?
8. Why do you think we are most likely to think of a reflection of water when we see a refraction of light from the sky on the road?
9. What do we think we see on the road?
10. What do we call what we see when our eyes seem to trick us like this?

# Coal

If you get land ___ is wet and boggy, and a warm, damp climate, ___ remains of plants and trees, leaves, ___ branches, etc. will ___ gather in the swampy ground. Instead ___ turning into compost, the water in the ground seals ___ the air. Therefore the plants cannot rot ___ properly, because they cannot get the oxygen ___ the air to do that.

The remains ___ plants can keep on gathering until they ___ many feet thick. If the swamp dries ___, these plant remains can be seen pressed ___ a brown damp mass of peat. In places ___ peat has formed, it is dug out ___ the ground and cut into flat slabs. These ___ are then dried, and make ___ fuel. Peat burns more slowly ___ wood, and therefore lasts ___.

If the peat gets covered over ___ soil and rocks, they are ___ heavy that the pressure forces ___ the water and gases from the peat. In the ___, only carbon is left. We know carbon ___ coal. Therefore, the peat has been ___ into coal.

Where there are several seams in ___ layers of other rocks, we know ___ a forest lived, formed peat, and then ___ covered with water. We think ___ the land may have sunk. Receding water left ___ thick mud, which formed shale ___ sandstone. Later, ___ the land was at the right height ___, forests grew until they were flooded ___ more.

We know that where we ___ coal, once forests grew there, and later, ___ covered that place.

*Now answer these questions in sentences:*

1. Why can't vegetation rot down properly in warm damp places?
2. What happens to the remains of plants in warm damp places?
3. If the swamp dries out, what is left?
4. What advantage has peat over wood as a fuel?
5. What happens to peat if it becomes covered with soil and rock?
6. What fuel is mostly carbon?
7. What could make land sink and rise again?
8. In the past, when land sank, what did it get covered with?
9. When the land rose out of the water again, what happened to it?
10. What can you tell about the way the earth has moved, and what grew on it, from seams of coal?

# Old Bottles

Many people nowadays enjoy collecting ___ bottles. They find them in dumps ___ estuaries. In the last century the majority ___ foods and beverages were sold ___ glass bottles. Plastic and polythene is ___ today where glass was used in the ___ century.

Dry tea was sold ___ bottles, toothpaste was bought in stone jars, cosmetics ___ in white pots. Fruit, tobacco, ___ polish, sweets and many other household ___ came in jars and bottles. ___ use, they were often thrown away. Bottles ___ held fizzy drinks had a glass marble ___ in their necks. The gas pressure from the ___ forced the marble up the neck ___ form a seal. To drink the ___ you had to push the marble ___. These bottles are not often ___ today, because so many were smashed ___ purpose to get the marble ___.

Old glass is usually coloured. ___ can be blue, brown, red, amber ___ white. The most common ___ is green. The glass usually contains air bubbles. The ___ do not usually have threads ___ the necks, because they were mainly sealed ___ corks. Their shapes and sizes ___, and they were often more interesting and attractive ___ the mass produced bottles we use ___.

*Now answer these questions in sentences:*

1. Where are many old bottles found?
2. Why were more things sold in bottles in the last century?
3. Name eight items that used to be sold in bottles, pots or jars?
4. Write down what containers these eight items are now sold in.
5. Instead of a stopper, how were bottles of fizzy drink sealed?
6. What sort of people do you suppose smashed the fizzy drink bottles, and why?
7. Name three things that might help you to know if a bottle is old.
8. What do you think is the attraction for many people in collecting old bottles?

# Mice

Many people ___ mice. Some people even scream and ___ on chairs. Some shudder. Those ___ rather like mice find it ___ to understand the feelings of ___ who do not.

However, quite apart ___ feelings about mice, it is generally ___ that mice are a health hazard. ___ contaminate food, and can make ___ very ill. This is why people ___ not want them in their ___, in particular in their kitchens.

Once, ___ we lived in the country, I went ___ get some raisins. There, sitting ___ the bottom of the packet, ___ a little mouse. We put ___ out of the back door! Then ___ had to replace the food ___ my larder, like rice and flour, ___ had been spoiled by the ___.

I think that mouse ___ we were soft, and brought ___ some friends! From then on ___ saw mice everywhere, darting ___ furniture and hiding in corners ___ we couldn't catch them. Those we ___ we let go further and ___ down the road. But they ___ came back!

The last straw came ___ a mouse ran over our feet ___ lunch time. We took in ___ stray kitten. An hour later, she ___ hadn't noticed the mouse, so we ___ it ourselves. We realised the ___ was ill. She had cat 'flu. ___ she recovered she lost her ___ of smell. She couldn't ___ a thing, let alone a mouse, ___ was far too slow to ___ one even if she had been ___ !

From the day she arrived, ___ never saw another mouse again. ___ we have a plague of cats ___ steal the food, race over ___ feet at mealtimes, and hide ___ chairs. . . . .

*Now answer these questions in sentences:*

1. For what reasons do people not want mice in their homes?
2. What damage did the mouse do?
3. In what ways were the mice a nuisance?
4. How did the people try to get rid of them?
5. What was the last straw?
6. What did the people do as a last resort?
7. What did the cat do, and why?
8. How did her illness affect the cat afterwards?
9. Why do you think the mice didn't come back?
10. Were the people better or worse off with cats or mice?

# Opening a Bank Account

It is easy to ___ a bank account nowadays. First ___ all you will have to give ___ bank personal details such as ___ and address. Then you must supply the ___ with a couple of references. ___ employer, or a friend ___ a bank account would be suitable ___ to act as referees. You also ___ give the bank specimens ___ your signature.

When the bank has ___ replies from your referees, you ___ be given a cheque book. Then, ___ of always carrying money around ___you, you can pay bills ___ cheque. When you need to ___ money from the bank you write ___ a cheque made payable to 'cash', and ___ it in at the bank. A cheque ___ account is called a current account. ___ can save your money in ___ deposit account, and get interest ___ the money you save.

There ___ other advantages in having a bank ___. You can have your salary ___ wages paid directly into the ___. You can also make arrangements ___ the bank to pay regular bills ___ you, like hire purchase payments. These ___ called standing orders. With ___ bankers card you can cash cheques ___ to £50 at any bank, ___ just the one you usually use. ___ are other services which the ___ will tell you about.

All in ___, a bank account has much ___ offer.

*Now answer these questions in sentences:*

1. What personal details must you give?
2. How many references do you usually need?
3. What sort of people are suitable to ask for references?
4. Why do you think the bank wants references?
5. Why does the bank want specimens of your signature?
6. What type of account is it where you have a cheque book?
7. What is the advantage of a deposit account over a current account if you want to save?
8. What is the advantage of a banker's card?
9. Name two other advantages in having a bank account.
10. What are standing orders?

# Christmas Shopping

One of my jobs when I ___ a girl, was to help my ___ with the shopping. On a Friday, ___ mother used to send me ___ the Co-op. about a mile away ___ the week's food. We were pretty poor ___, and the week's groceries used ___ come to less than a pound. My mother ___ to send me with a doll's ___ to put the food in, and I ___ go after tea.

On this particular occasion, ___ few weeks after my seventh birthday, ___ was sent on Christmas Eve ___ the pram, a list, and a pound ___ to buy the food we needed ___ Christmas.

I remember standing in ___ queue, with the pound in ___ hand, feeling very grown up. ___ I got to the counter, I ___ the pound note had gone. The ___ was searched but it couldn't ___ found. Someone had either taken it ___ my hand, or, if I'd dropped ___, from the floor while I ___ in the queue.

I will ___ forget that walk home. I was ___, because I knew there was ___ more money to buy the food ___ needed.

My mother was in ___ kitchen when I opened the door ___ the warm, lighted room and blurted ___ the bad news. Her face ___ terrible. She didn't need to ___ me off or shout at me. She ___ on her coat and raced ___ the shop on her bike. The ___ had not been found.

To ___ for the food that Christmas, my ___ had to pawn my new bike. ___ was nearly Easter before she ___ saved enough money to get my ___ back again.

*Now answer these questions in sentences:*

1. How old was the girl?
2. What day in the year did this happen?
3. What job did the girl do every week?
4. What three things did she take to the shop every week?
5. When did she notice the money was missing?
6. What was done to try and find the money?
7. What do you think probably happened to the pound?
8. Where was the girl's mother when she got home?
9. Why did her mother not shout at her?
10. How did the family get money to buy food?
11. How long did the girl have to wait to get her bike back?
12. Why did she have to wait that long?
13. Whose fault was it the money was lost, and why?

# Apples

Originally, wild apples were ___ from the apples we know today. ___ Afghanistan wild apple forests can ___ be found. The fruits of these ___ are sour, and rather like crab ___. These apples were developed to ___ sweeter, larger fruit, by people ___ the Near East and India.

The first apples ___ not come to Britain until ___ the Norman Conquest. French noblemen ___ to cultivate apple orchards. The costard ___ an early apple, with rather a sharp and ___ very sweet taste. They were ___ into costard sauce and costard puddings. ___ original apple sellers were ___ as costard-mongers. This name became ___ to costermongers, which now ___ a travelling seller of fruit, vegetables ___ fish.

Now, there are more ___ six thousand distinct varieties of ___. Commercial growers like to grow ___ all the same size, with ___ yields and good keeping properties. ___ means that you will taste very ___ other apples apart from ___ Golden Delicious, which is the most widely ___.

*Now answer these questions in sentences:*

1. Where can wild apples still be found?
2. How are wild apples different to cultivated apples?
3. Who first cultivated wild apples?
4. Who brought the first apples to Britain?
5. What was the name of the favourite early apple?
6. How was it used?
7. What was the name of the people who sold it?
8. What has the name changed to over the centuries?
9. What does the name now mean?
10. How many apple varieties are there now?
11. What is the most common apple today?
12. What do commercial growers look for when growing apples?

# Penguins

Penguins are only ___ in the Southern Hemisphere, but ___ not live only on frozen ___ and sea. They like cool sea ___ a rule, and live in Antarctica round ___ coasts of South America, Africa ___ Australasia. There ___ two exceptions, the Peruvian penguin ___ lives on the coast of Chile, ___ the Galapagos penguin which ___ on the Galapagos Islands, ___ to the Equator.

Penguins ___ fly. Their wings have evolved ___ flippers, which make them superb ___. A penguin's body is covered ___ a layer of blubber, which ___ it to float as well ___ keep it warm. Penguins live ___ colonies, never on their ___.

At nesting time the ___ spread out evenly over a rocky headland. ___ male brings pebbles to the ___ who spreads them round her ___ a nest shape. From when ___ leave the sea they do not eat. ___ about two or three weeks, ___ the eggs are laid, the female ___ back to the sea to feed. The ___ sits on the eggs until she ___, two or three weeks later. ___ he goes to the sea ___ feed. After about seven weeks, ___ chicks hatch, and the parents ___ turns to feed them.

In ___ Antarctic, the penguins' main ___ are the leopard seals in the ___ and the great skua ___ land. This is a sea bird which ___ seize any chance to steal ___ egg or a chick.

*Now answer these questions in sentences:*

1. Where are penguins mainly found?
2. Which penguins are found outside the Antarctic?
3. In which hemisphere do all penguins live?
4. Why can penguins not fly?
5. What does the layer of blubber do?
6. Are penguins designed for land, sea or air?
7. Do penguins like company?
8. Where do penguins lay their eggs?
9. What are their nests made from?
10. What parts do the males and females play in nest building?
11. For how long is the female hungry?
12. For how long is the male hungry?
13. How long does it take for the eggs to hatch?
14. How are the chicks looked after?
15. What do the penguins fear most on land and sea?

# The Mosquito

A female mosquito or gnat ___ her eggs on top of stagnant ___. In a day or two the eggs ___ into squirming larvae which you can ___ on ponds or water butts in summer. ___ larvae breathe by pushing a long tube ___ above the surface of the water. Sticklebacks eat ___, but a more effective way of controlling mosquitoes ___ to spray the water with paraffin, ___ suffocates the larvae.

If the larvae is ___ killed or eaten, it becomes ___ pupa. In a few days the ___ of the pupa splits and a mosquito ___ out. It rests in the sun ___ a few minutes, using the cast-off ___ as a raft, and then flies ___. It is now a full grown ___ and its life will last ___ two weeks.

Mosquitoes are found ___, from the tropics to the Arctic.

*Now answer these questions in sentences:*

1. Where are mosquitoes found?
2. Where does the female lay her eggs?
3. What do the eggs hatch into?
4. How can you kill the larvae?
5. What does the larvae turn into?
6. How does the mosquito get out?
7. How long does an adult mosquito live?
8. Write down the four stages in the life of a mosquito, from the egg to the adult mosquito.

# Riding at Sixteen

In 1971 the law ___ changed. Until that time, when ___ were sixteen you could ride ___ motorbike. Because of the high accident ___ the age limit for riding ___ motorbike or motor scooter was ___ to seventeen. Now, sixteen year ___ can only ride a moped.

A ___ is defined by law ___ having an engine of not ___ than 50 ccs as well as pedals. ___ car licence qualifies you to ___ a moped. If you have ___ already got a licence, you must ___ a provisional licence.

You can ___ a passenger if you have ___ full driving licence and the moped ___ fitted with footrests for the ___. You may not ride your moped ___ a motorway. After three years you ___ have your moped tested by ___ Department of the Environment.

Mopeds used ___ be more or less bicycles ___ an engine tacked on somewhere. Nowadays ___ look more like motorbikes and ___ like bicycles than they did.

*Now answer these questions in sentences:*

1. When was the law concerning sixteen year olds changed?
2. In what way was the law changed?
3. What is a moped?
4. What sort of licence do you need to drive a moped if you are (a) a sixteen year old, (b) a car driver?
5. What two things must you have in order to carry a passenger?
6. When must you have your moped tested by the D.o.E.?
7. Can you drive a moped on all roads?
8. How has the appearance of mopeds changed over the years?

# Cobbles and Setts

Have you ___ noticed cobbles and setts in ___ parts of towns? Before tarmac, roads ___ often surfaced with them. Cobbles ___ unshaped stones, whereas setts are carved, and ___ be made of wood or stone.

Sett-knapping, ___ art of cutting the setts, ___ a dying skill. It used to ___ part of the apprenticeship ___ highway staff, as was the skill ___ laying the stones to avoid wobble. Maintenance ___ now a serious problem. As a ___ of Bradford Council said, '___ masons wouldn't recognise a knapper's hammer ___ you hit them over the head ___ it!'

People who would like ___ see these old roads preserved ___ that they have the effect ___ slowing traffic down, and are ___ as good as ramps and strips ___ many councils install nowadays.

These ___ roads, because of legal complications, ___ not protected by the Department ___ the Environment. Their future ___ threatened because of this, and the ___ of setters. It is likely ___ there will be less of ___ in the future acting as reminders ___ our urban history.

*Now answer these questions in sentences:*

1. Where do you find cobbles and setts?
2. What are cobbles?
3. What are setts?
4. What are roads usually surfaced with now?
5. What is the name given to the art of cutting setts?
6. Name one of the tools a knapper might use.
7. What would happen to the setts if they are laid by someone who is inexperienced?
8. Name at least one town which has setts or cobbles.
9. What practical argument is put forward for keeping these old roads in towns?
10. Can you write down any other reasons for keeping these roads?
11. Why does the D.o.E. not protect these roads?
12. Why are there likely to be fewer of these roads in the future?

# Shifting Populations

For as long as there ____ been records, people have moved about ____ one part of the world to the ____. Britain has received many immigrants, and has also ____ many people to other countries.

In the first thousand ____ A.D. there were four important movements ____ Britain. These came ____ the Romans, the Saxons, the Danes (Vikings) ____ the Normans (from France). All ____ people helped to shape the Britain ____ know now. Their influence can ____ be found in the English language, and ____ buildings and roads.

In the sixteenth century, many ____ left Britain to go to North America. ____ were the English Puritans who went ____ there was not enough religious freedom ____. In the seventeenth century, Huguenots came ____ Britain because there was not enough religious ____ in France.

In later years, many people ____ England to colonise Canada, Australia, New Zealand, South Africa. ____ went to the United States. Millions of Irish ____ left Ireland after years of famine to ____ new lives in America and Canada. Many Jews ____ the Russian Empire because of racial persecution ____ the nineteenth century, and left Germany for the ____ reason this century, settling in Britain. Millions ____ people were left homeless after the last ____. Half a million of these refugees ____ to Britain. And since the war ____ have come from the Commonwealth.

In all ____ population movements, there are strong reasons ____ moving. People feel they do ____ have a happy future in their country, because of lack of food, opportunity, ____ political or religious oppression. ____ they want a better future for ____ children, they are prepared to uproot ____ to make a new start.

*Now answer these questions in sentences:*

1. What are the usual reasons people migrate?
2. What immigrants did Britain receive from 0–1,000 A.D.?
3. What effect did they have on the culture of the country?
4. Make two lists, of the people who left Britain and the people who came to Britain from 1000 A.D. to now. Write down who they are and why they moved.
5. Choose a country which interests you, and suggest advantages and disadvantages of emigrating to it.

# Windscreen

As the car is travelling down a country ___, a lorry scatters mud and stones ___ it passes between the roadworks ___ the car. There is a sharp crack ___ a stone hits the windscreen ___ bounces away. Suddenly the people ___ the car are aware of ___ crackling sound, and they realise ___ is the car windscreen breaking. Spreading ___ the place where the stone ___ it, the glass is cracking ___ ripples from this centre. The first ___ are long and wavy, enclosing long, rough rectangles ___ glass. Then these long pieces of glass ___ across, dividing the big pieces ___ three or four smaller pieces which ___ almost cube-shaped. The pattern is beautiful; ___ grows, minute by minute, until the entire ___ is one intricate, lacy network. ___ half an hour the impact of the ___ can still be heard, as ___ resonating windscreen fills every last fragment ___ the echo of its ruin.

*Now answer these questions in sentences:*

1. Where was the car when the windscreen cracked?
2. Where was the lorry?
3. What caused the crack in the windscreen?
4. What is the first sign of the windscreen breaking?
5. How do the cracks move across the windscreen?
6. What shape is the cracked glass to begin with?
7. How does the shape of the glass change?
8. Why do you think the writer described the windscreen as a network?
9. How long does the sound of cracking go on for?
10. Why does the writer call the cracking an echo?

# Laws

Laws are made to ____ the interests of the majority ____ any group. They protect that ____. If most people did ____ agree with a particular law ____ would fall into disuse. It ____ be too hard to make ____ many people stick to it.

For ____, during the Hundred Years' War ____ was a law which said ____ all men over a certain age ____ to practise archery on a Sunday. ____ was obviously useful at the ____, but when it was no ____ necessary, after the war, the law ____ not observed any more. If ____ people do not support it, it ____ impossible to enforce. Another example ____ a law which has fallen ____ disuse is the one which ____ it illegal for children to ____ more than ten hours a ____ in factories.

Often laws are unpopular ____ some people at first. The above law ____ have been unpopular with factory ____! After all, every law makes ____ do something, or someone stop ____ something!

Laws affect many aspects ____ our lives. Laws which affect us ____ the standards of housing and food, and the ____ of noise and dirt in ____ atmosphere. Behaviour on the roads, safety ____ public buildings ____ schools and factories, and the type ____ hospitals and schools available, ____ many other areas affected by ____.

*Now answer these questions in sentences:*

1. Why are laws made?
2. Whom do they protect?
3. If people do not agree with a law, what happens to it?
4. Give two examples of laws which have fallen into disuse.
5. Why are some laws unpopular?
6. Which areas of our lives do laws affect?
7. Can you think of any behaviour not mentioned in the passage affected by laws?

# Drinks

There are ___ types of drink on sale these days. Often the labels ___ confusing. What they contain is controlled ___ law. Here is a description ___ the eight most common types of fruit ___.

By law, any drink you buy ___ has 'fruit juice' written on the ___ must contain 100% fruit juice. An example is orange ___.

A fruit squash ___ different. It is a concentrated fruit juice ___ must contain 25% of fruit juice before ___ is diluted, a minimum amount ___ sugar, and a maximum ___ of saccharin. (Saccharin is ___ chemical sweetener.)

A fruit barley water, ___ lemon barley, is also considered to ___ a fruit squash. It must ___ barley in it, and it ___ have 15% of fruit juice. You ___ it with water like a squash.

A fruit crush ___ a squash that has already ___ diluted. It must contain 5% ___ juice.

If the label says ___ the tin or bottle contains ___ fruit drink, then it means ___ only about 10% of the liquid ___ from fruit. Even less of this is ___ juice, because the flesh and peel ___ pulped and used as well ___ the juice.

A low calorie drink ___ the same amount of fruit ___ an ordinary fruit drink, but has ___ calories.

If you buy a fruit flavoured ___, or an ade, like orangeade, ___ it contains no fruit at all. These ___ are usually fizzy, and artificial flavourings ___ them their taste.

All these drinks, except ___ fruit juices, contain flavouring, preservatives and colouring.

*Now follow these instructions:*

1. Write down the names of the eight types of drink, and give an example of each.
2. Write out the types of drink which contain fruit juice, starting with the drink which contains least fruit juice.
3. Write out the names of the drinks which contain at least 10% of fruit juice.
4. Write down which additives each type of drink may contain.

# Wheat

Wheat contains many nutrients necessary ___ health. The brown outer layer ___ the wheat contains the bran. This ___ vital for the smooth working of the digestive ___. It is not considered a food in ___ own right, but provides necessary fibre ___ the digestive system. There are many illnesses ___ are caused by too little fibre ___ the diet, such as diverticulitis and ___ bowel disorders. White flour contains no bran, ___ the white centre or endosperm. Endosperm ___ starch, which gives energy. A surplus ___ starch is stored as fat.

In the middle ___ the grain is the wheat germ, which contains protein ___ body building Vitamin E, most of the eighteen B Vitamins, and mineral salts. ___ E is necessary for the digestion ___ fats, and helps in heart disease ___ some nervous troubles. The B vitamins ___ vital for a whole range of body functions ___ are vital for health, as are small amounts ___ mineral salts. White flour contains no ___ germ.

Bread made from white flour contains ___ the starchy part of the wheat. The ___ contains the compulsory additions of powdered chalk, iron compound ___ two of the B vitamins. It also may ___ bleaching agents, improvers, extenders ___ preservatives.

*Now answer these questions in sentences:*

1. What is the name of the outer layer of the wheat?
2. What is it necessary for?
3. What illnesses are caused by too little fibre in the diet?
4. What is the name for the starchy middle?
5. Why is starch necessary?
6. Which part of the wheat contains the vitamins?
7. Why is protein needed in the diet?
8. Which vitamins not in white flour are in whole wheat flour?
9. Which parts of the wheat are not in white flour?
10. What must white bread have in it, apart from flour?
11. What may white bread have in it, in addition to the compulsory additives?
12. Which do you think is better for you, white bread or whole wheat bread?

# Baths Advertisement

**BOROUGH ___ BRADLAKE**

**BATHS DEPARTMENT**

Applications ___ invited for the following posts ___ Bradlake Outdoor Swimming ___.
All posts will be terminated ___ the end of the current summer ___ on September 4th.

POOL ATTENDANTS

___ should be strong swimmers, preferably ___ a Bronze Medallion Award.

BASKET ROOM ATTENDANTS/CASHIERS

Applicants ___ the above posts must have a pleasant ___ and experience in dealing ___ members of the public. ___ for the post of cashier ___ have experience in handling ___.
Succesful applicants will be ___ to work on a shift basis. ___ forms are available from The Baths Manager,
c/o ___ Baths,
Bradlake.

*Now answer these questions in sentences:*

1. Which Borough is advertising?
2. Which posts are available?
3. Where are the vacancies?
4. Are these jobs permanent or temporary?
5. What qualifications are necessary for the job of Pool attendant?
6. What qualifications are necessary for the job of Cashier?
7. What qualifications are necessary for the job of Basket Room Attendant?
8. Can you think of any disadvantages to any of these jobs?
9. What types of people do you think might be interested in applying for any of these jobs?
10. What must you do if you are interested in any of these jobs?

# Summer Cycling

Cycling in the English countryside ___ be a great pleasure, especially in ___ summer. Roads, familiar by car, ___ completely different when travelled ___ bike. For instance, a road ___ seems relatively flat has a surprising number ___ hills to a cyclist. Villages and houses ___ seem merely pretty when glimpsed ___ a car window are much ___ interesting from a saddle. Because the pace is ___, the cyclist sees much ___. Each turn of the ___ brings a changing scene, but slowly enough ___ the cyclist to enjoy the way ___ scene flows into another.

Instead ___ catching sight of some activity ___ seems frozen for ever, the ___ sees these activities as scenes, rather than snapshots.

Above ___, there are the smells and sounds ___ countryside which cannot ___ appreciated from a car. ___ a bike moves virtually silently, ___ cyclist sees many wild creatures ___ about their natural activities rather ___ seeing them flattened at the ___ of a road.

As a treat ___ all the senses, cycling takes ___ beating.

*Now answer these questions in sentences:*

1. Give two ways in which travelling by bike and car is different.
2. Why does a cyclist see more?
3. How can the same scene be appreciated differently, depending on how you travel?
4. Which two senses are stimulated when cycling, which aren't when travelling by car?
5. Compare the views a cyclist and a motorist would have of the wild life in the countryside.
6. The writer talks about cycling in summer. Which season do you enjoy cycling in most, and why?

# The History of Flying

Aviation has a short history, ___ it started only in 1903 ___ the Wright brothers built their first ___. Many people then became involved ___ aircraft development whose ___ are still remembered today, such ___ Sopwith, Vickers, Bristol, Avro ___ Handley Page.

The First World ___ saw aircraft used for reconnaissance ___ first, and as fighters towards the ___ of the war. The Germans developed the 'Fokker', ___ the British the Sopwith 'Camel' as fighter ___.

The period between the ___ saw the development of planes capable ___ flying much longer distances. Alcock and Brown ___ the Atlantic in 1919; in 1927 Lindbergh flew ___ New York to Paris, and ___ 1931 Wiley Post flew round the ___ in less than 9 days.

Bigger ___ better bombers and fighters were ___ for the Second World War. Best remembered ___ the Spitfire and Hurricane fighters, ___ the Wellington and Lancaster bombers, ___ the Mosquito used for reconnaissance, fighting and ___. In comparison to the aircraft ___ for the First World War, when the Handley Page ___ fly at 80 mph with 16 × 112lb. bombs, ___ aircraft developed by the early forties ___ vastly superior. For instance, the Lancaster ___ carry 14,000lbs. for 1,660 ___, and the Mosquito flew at ___ of over 400 mph.

Since the War, aircraft ___ has proceeded at a similar phenomenal ___, leading, amongst other developments, ___ to the Harriers, Jumbo Jets and Concorde.

*Now answer these questions in sentences:*

1. Who were the first people to fly?
2. What three uses were planes developed for in war time?
3. Which planes are best remembered for each of these uses in both wars?
4. Illustrate the development of aircraft by giving two examples of improved range, capacity and speed.
5. What emphasis is given to development of aircraft capabilities in peace time?
6. Give examples of post Second World War aircraft development.

# New Space Discoveries

Some new discoveries have ___ made recently by astronomers ___ the Royal Observatory, Edinburgh. Using ___ giant telescope camera on a remote mountain top, ___ believe they have discovered a previously ___ dwarf galaxy near the Milky Way. Other galaxies ___ at the edge of the observable universe ___ also been discovered.

The photographs, taken ___ the UK Schmidt telescope, have ___ funded by the Science Research Council, and ___ part of a systematic survey ___ the southern skies. These new ___ are the first to be discovered ___ twenty years.

The telescope ___ see farther into the universe ___ any other survey telescope. Photographs ___ established that another galaxy previously ___ to be exceptionally young, is in ___ a much older galaxy.

It is also ___ that the photographs might establish ___ the next year whether space ___ 'flat' or 'round'. This would be ___ important step forward in our knowledge ___ the universe, as was Columbus' proof ___ the earth was round.

*Now answer these questions in sentences:*

1. Who has made these discoveries?
2. What equipment was used?
3. Where was the equipment sited?
4. What has been discovered?
5. Who has paid for the research?
6. What was being surveyed when these discoveries were made?
7. When were the last known galaxies discovered?
8. What additional information about a known galaxy has been discovered?
9. What is it hoped to establish in the near future?
10. In what ways is the expected proof about the universe similar to Columbus' discovery?